SIMPLIFIED ECHO DOT MANUAL FOR BEGINNERS

Updated Amazon Echo Dot 2nd and 3rd Gen User Guide for Seniors

With Alexa

BRIAN A. LAKE

Copyright© 2019

Dedicated

To my daughter, Queen.

AKNOWLEDGEMENT

I want to say a big thank you to my friends at *DockYard Inc.* for their valuable support.

Table of Contents

Chapter 1 9

Introducing Amazon Echo devices 9

Chapter 2 31

How to set up your Amazon Echo Dot
and other Echo devices 31

    Download Alexa app 33

    Connect Echo Device to a power
    source 36

    Connect your Echo device to a
    Wi-Fi 38

    Update Wi-Fi Settings for your
    Echo device 40

    How to set up Alexa voice profile
    on your Echo device 42

Setting up the voice profile through screen prompts 45

How to setup music on your Echo device 48

Connect your Echo device to Bluetooth speaker 50

Chapter 3 54

20 Alexa skills you can access with Amazon Echo devices 54

How to add Alexa skills 58

Manage your Synchrony Bank account with Amazon store Card skill 60

Enable Alexa to manage your Capital One accounts on Echo device 63

Ordering Pizza through Alexa on your Echo device 65

How to connect your smart home devices to Amazon Echo 69

Use guided discovery to enable a smart home device on Alexa 72

Use Alexa skill to catch up on the news (Set up Flash Briefings) 73

Setup calling & messaging skill in Alexa communication 75

Set up your Uber account so Alexa can get you a ride 78

Get your Sports Scores on Echo through voice request to Alexa 80

Monitor the Stock Market 84

How to Track your packages with Alexa 87

Secure your Alexa privacy 93

Try meditation with Alexa on Echo device 95

No end to Alexa Skills 98

DISCLAIMER 100

ABOUT THE AUTHOR 101

Chapter 1

Introducing Amazon Echo devices

Amazon Echo devices are loudspeakers with some skills that enable you to do many things by mere talking, or with your voice, without lifting a finger. They've got some digital sense to help you make phone calls, refine musical sounds, tell the weather and listen to news updates, all hands-free.

The Echo can give you these, and many more, digital assistance because it carries Alexa, the famous Amazon brand of artificial intelligence (AI).

With Alexa in the Echo, you can use your voice to turn on/off kitchen lights, lock or unlock smart doors, trigger or disable compatible home alarm systems and control multi-room audio equipment. Some premium Echo devices come with web browser skills and high-resolution touchscreens that let you perform most smartphone functions, again, without lifting a finger.

If you don't own any model of Echo device yet, it may not be too long before you get one. Just about everyone is going for them. As at the close of 2019, Echo devices had taken Amazon's artificial intelligence into more than 100 million homes, mostly in the United States, Mexico, Western Europe, Australia and New Zealand.

There're signs that the Echo-Alexa alliance will show up in more homes and regions in 2020, and beyond. Alexa is gaining thousands of new skills, in addition to those it already has. It's being installed in more types of devices, while more manufacturers make thousands of new home equipment that can be operated by voice command to Alexa.

You can correctly predict that the future is bright for Alexa and the other artificial intelligence software like Google Assistant and Apple's Siri.

So, again, if you haven't picked up one Amazon Echo device yet, you can bet it won't be long before you do. And when it's time for you to pick up one of them, you might find it a bit challenging to know which device is best for you. The reason is, there're many types of Echo-Alexa devices in circulation, offering near-similar services, with varying degrees of efficiency.

You'll benefit by reading through the lineup presented below, to get acquainted with these amazing tech equipment. Then, you can choose wisely from among the dozens on parade, and also optimize your user experience of the model you choose.

It's important to know that no model of these devices in the market has an internal battery. You'd be surprised that Amazon makes them without batteries. In fact, the only Echo device that ever had a battery of its own, the Amazon Echo Tap, was discontinued in December 2018. And so, all the models currently on sale need to stay connected to a charger, or a battery base, while they work.

This is a problem for the product in Africa and other regions of the world faced with epileptic power supply.

Let's take a quick look at some of the Amazon Echo devices in circulation as at the close of 2019:

1. **<u>Amazon Echo 2019</u>**

The Echo of 2019 mimicked the original hardware design when Echo's beta version was released on November 6, 2014, and when it became widely available in the US on June 23, 2015. Subsequent revisions came with adjustments of one or more functions of the original product, sometimes, to make the device more affordable to consumers.

The basic features included voice interaction, music playback, setting alarms, streaming podcast, playing audiobooks and making to-do-list. They provide news updates and real-time information about weather, traffic situation and sports scores. Echo devices also serve as a home automation hub.

The baseline Echo has undergone vast improvements over the years. The third generation (2019) version focused on the improvement of the audio quality, as well as affordability.

It incorporates the improved audio quality of the Amazon Echo Plus, but downgraded the smart home automation hub, in order to reduce its selling price. So, the 2019 Echo version is a cheaper Echo Plus, at $79.99 on the Amazon stores.

2. **Echo Plus, second generation**

If you're looking for the most functional portable Alexa hardware, the Echo Plus looks like one. It offers louder sounds, of more apparent quality, and comes with a heat sensor that can initiate specific actions based on the temperature of your home. Its ability to do smart things is enhanced by inbuilt Zigbee, which Alexa uses to find and connect to all Alexa compatible devices in the house. You can then use voice interaction to control the linked devices, be they light bulbs, microwaves, alarms and smart door locks.

If you hope to buy many smart home appliances, Echo Plus is the version for you. So, you can willingly part with more bucks to get Echo Plus at $149.99.

3. The Echo Show (2nd Gen)

But then, the Echo Plus isn't the costliest Alexa hardware in town. That prize, without a contest, goes to Echo Show in its second revision. This version comes with a 10-inch (about 25 cm) high definition display, twice the screen size of the original Echo Show. It also stepped forth with enhanced sound quality and inbuilt web browser that relies on voice command to do much of what you usually do on a smartphone or laptop.

And so, with Echo Show, you can tell Alexa to open Firefox, and the browser is launched on your Echo Show screen. And you can type the URL of any website using the onscreen keyboard, and the website would appear on your screen. This 2018 Amazon Echo upgrade represented a massive improvement in the Echo-Alexa partnership. It offers more powerful speakers, more substantial touch screen functionality, home automation hub and better everything else that the Echo has.

You can agree that it's a good Echo device choice, at $229.99, if you aren't already carrying a credit card of $7,200, said to be the average card debt for an American household. Wise persons do not buy premium models, only to sink deeper into the cesspool of debt.

4. Amazon Echo Dot (third generation)

For anyone already neck-deep in debt, the star Echo device at the moment might be the Amazon Echo Dot, now in its third revision. It's the most affordable of them all, at a mere $24.99 on Amazon. It's also the most portable, being only the size of a hockey puck.

As the third and latest revision of the Amazon Echo wireless speaker series, the Dot delivers better sound output than its predecessors. The sturdy fabric cover and colour options of charcoal, grey, sandstone and plum, make the Echo Dot a pleasant piece of equipment inside the house.

As 2019 was winding down, the 3rd Amazon Echo Dot was selling better than any smart speaker in the market. Small and very portable, the latest Echo Dot is easy to set up and integrate with compatible devices. It's got clear audio quality and enhanced Alexa app performance.

5. Echo Dot with Clock

The addition of a digital clock on the Echo Dot expands its functions. For an extra cost of $10, you get the Dot that offers you a table clock, with colorful display of both time and weather information. This is in addition to a million other tasks that you can achieve, faster and smarter, by merely talking to Alexa in the cylinder.

6. The Echo Studio

The Studio is another high-end Echo device, which offers upscale sound reproduction experience. It's compatible with Dolby Atmos surround sound setup. The Echo Studio leads in precise sound effect placement and covers the sound frequency range better than any other Echo-Alexa device. On voice command, it performs every other primary task of Echo-Alexa devices. It justifies its relatively high price tag of $199.99.

7. Amazon Echo Show 8

If you love the high-end Echo Show, but can't go for it because of budget constraints, you can settle for Echo Show 8. This version of smart wireless speaker is 2 inches smaller than the upscale Echo Show and much less expensive. Tech reviewers see it as a near-perfect balance between performance, size and price. It looks good for $79.99.

8. Echo Show 5

This version of Echo Show is even smaller and less expensive. It offers a 5.5 inches display, with a resolution of 960 pixels by 480 pixels, a 1MP high definition camera. While retaining all the Alexa voice commands, the Echo Show 5 offers a trademark touchscreen and web browsing ability. It looks like a top-pick Alexa hardware, for $59.99 on Amazon.

9. Amazon Echo Buds

The Echo bud is a wireless earphone that houses Alexa, the first wire-free earpiece from Amazon. It's quite remarkable in that, it's capable of working with rival digital assistants like Apple's Siri and Google Assistant. Depending on your setup, you can summon any of the three AIs, using their activation words.

You would not expect the exceptional sound quality of Echo Show or Echo Studio from a mere earphone, but if you want something to stick to the ear and, through it, use voice command to perform a whole of digital tasks, then the versatile Echo Bud is your best bet.

They aren't cheap at $130 apiece, but they offer unrivalled convenience of easy carriage, mobility and options of three great artificial bits of intelligence.

10. **Echo Dot for Kids**

Amazon knows that kids have special needs. So, their Echo Dot version is full of kid-friendly features, including unlimited Free Time that connects children to a thousand audiobooks, thousands of songs, appropriate games and skills. Echo Dot for kids also have features that let parents set activity and time limits for their kids, and to review compliance with such limits. Made to absorb shock, the kids' version comes with a two-year warranty, with Amazon committing to replacing them if they break within the warranty period. At $69.99, Echo Dot for children isn't the least expensive of the pack, but their customized features and beautiful rainbow and reliable blue color options make them good tech toys for your kids.

11. **The Echo Glow**

Another Echo device for children is the Echo Glow. This is a dazzling device that can display different colorful lights in response to user's voice command. For instance, the kid user can ask Alexa to change the Glow's color, and it does so. The Glow doesn't have all the features, nor is it able to perform all the tasks that Amazon Echo devices are known for. Instead, it's more like a smart lamp for the children's room.

12.   **Echo smart gadgets**

Amazon has gone ahead to produce several gadgets that serve as adapters. These help you to enable Alexa on home appliances not compatible with it. For instance, the Amazon Smart Plug can connect to Echo Dot and let you operate your non-smart coffee pot with a voice command. In that case, the smart plug will enable Alexa to operate the on/off switches of the coffee brewer. You can say, **'Alexa, turn off the coffee pot,'** and it's done, though the coffee isn't initially smart.

The Echo Input is another adapter that lets you extend Alexa support to nearby loudspeakers that aren't initially smart. Through a Bluetooth or an audio cable, you can enable Alexa to operate third party speakers that help sound quality improvements in an environment in which the Echo speakers might not satisfy the needs of the moment.

Other Echo-Alexa products that you may wish to check out are the Echo Frames, which puts Alexa skills on your eyeglasses; Echo Loop that makes Alexa available on your finger ring and Amazon Basics Microwave oven that you can operate with voice instructions to Alexa.

Chapter 2

How to set up your Amazon Echo Dot and other Echo devices

Let's say that you eventually picked up one of the Amazon Echo devices, perhaps, the third-generation Echo Dot. You'll need to set it up or prepare it to work for you. The first thing you need to do to get an Echo device up and running is to download or update Alexa app on your mobile device.

Download Alexa app

You're well aware that Echo devices work with Alexa app. In fact, without the Alexa app, your Echo Dot will be no smarter than a real hockey puck, in both look and function. It's Alexa that makes Echo devices smart. You download the app on smartphones or tablets running on Android 5.1 or newer; iOS 11 or higher and Amazon Fire OS 5.3 and later.

Of course, you're familiar with the process of downloading apps. You open the app store on your device, could be the Google Play Store, Apple store or Windows app store, whatever. Then search for Alexa app, download and install. But if you want to download to a PC, the process would be different. You'll need to connect to a Wi-Fi, then go to Amazon Alexa website to download the app you need to operate your new Echo device.

When the app has finished installing or updating, as the case may be:

- Launch the **Alexa app** by clicking its blue icon
- Click the **Settings** icon, consisting of three lines, the last of which is smaller than the first two
- Select **Add Devices**

- Choose **Amazon Echo**, then the very model of the Echo product that you want to add
- Click on the model and wait for your phone to locate the device (when it's plugged to power and switched on) and pair with it.

Connect Echo Device to a power source

As noted earlier, no Echo model has its own battery. They all have to be plugged and stay so, to work. The Echo Tap, which had a battery, was curiously retired by Amazon in December 2018.

Well, you may not feel the absence of a battery, though, since these devices are primarily made for indoor use, so they can always stay connected to power outlet. You can always access Alexa skills with smartphones that are with everywhere you go.

When you first connect your new Echo to a power source, its ring of light turns blue to confirm it's now live. When the light changes to orange, Alexa is getting ready to say a greeting to you, and subsequently, tell you to proceed with the setup process.

Connect your Echo device to a Wi-Fi

It's quite obvious why you need to hook up your new Echo device to a Wi-Fi network. Every support that Alexa needs to perform its task resides in the Cloud. So, you need to be online for it to work. You also need to know that your new Echo equipment will not work on ad-hoc or peer-to-peer Wi-Fi networks. It can only work on dual-band Wi-Fi networks within the speed range of 2.4 GHz to 5 GHz.

Assuming you're on a standard network:

- Open your **Alexa** app
- View the available network and select the one you use
- If you own more than one Echo device, go to menu
- Select **Alexa Device**, then choose the new Echo you're now setting up
- Under the **Wireless** tab, you'll select your Wi-Fi network

After connecting, it'll be helpful to save your Wi-Fi network passcode on Amazon. You'll be needing it when you want to pair up your Echo with other smart devices or when you want to set up a new piece of Echo. Again, if the Wi-Fi you're connecting is open access public network, it'll be unwise to save your password there.

Update Wi-Fi Settings for your Echo device

You use your mobile Alexa app to update Wi-Fi settings on Echo Dot or any other model of this device. And this is how you do it:

- Open Alexa app
- Select **Devices**
- Choose **Echo and Alexa**
- Then choose your Echo device
- Next to **Wi-Fi network**, tap **Change**

- Then follow onscreen instructions to adjust the things you want to tweak.

What if your network is hidden, or does not appear among those listed? You'll have to scroll down and choose the option to **Add a Network**, to **Rescan**. Either way, you'll be able to see your network.

How to set up Alexa voice profile on your Echo device

You know that Echo devices work through your voice commands to Alexa. So, the first thing you do when your Echo device is up and running is to create your file profile. You need to teach Alexa to recognize your voice. And if they're others in the family, each member needs to have a voice profile with Alexa so that each person can receive personalized assistance from Alexa.

To create a voice account with Alexa:

- Open the Alexa app on your mobile device
- On the menu page, select **Settings**
- Then, choose **Accounts**
- Tap on **Your Voice**, and hit **Begin** to start the training.

Alexa is capable and willing to guide you through the voice learning process. You say something like *"Alexa, learn my voice."* Alexa will go ahead to guide you verbally on how to set up your voice profile.

What if you own two or more Alexa-enabled devices, say, more than one Amazon Echo devices in the house? Then, you'll have to choose one of them for the voice training exercise.

You'll do well to switch off the microphones of any Echo equipment not being used for the training. Good thing is, once you set up your voice profile on one of them, the rest will recognize and obey it.

Setting up the voice profile through screen prompts

Let's say you chose not to follow Alexa verbal guidance to set up your voice profile. You'll then have to follow onscreen prompting to arrive at the same destination. The app will show you some phrases.

And you'll need to say them out loud as they show up. If you stumble on any phrase, just tap Try Again, to enable you repeat it. When you've gone through the phrases, tap Complete, and a confirmation message from Alexa will let you know you've done a good job.

While teaching Alexa to know your voice, do minimize background noise. Also, place your Echo device at least 8 inches away from the wall. And finally, place the Echo device exactly where it'll always stay in the house, while you sit or stand in the place where you'll be interacting with Alexa always.

Despite Alexa's congratulatory message, you may want to test the set up immediately after setup, to confirm it has learnt your voice. But you've got to give it some 15 minutes gap, the approximate time it takes to master your voice after the training altogether.

You can then ask, *"Alexa, who am I?"* If all is well, Alexa will say something like "I'm talking with (William J. Johnson). And if your name isn't pronounced correctly, you may need to seek help from Amazon help center.

- Using the Alexa app, tap **Help & Feedback**
- Then select **Send Feedback**
- On the drop-down menu, select your device & the problem
- Then write a complaint in the textbox and await suggestions from the help desk.

How to setup music on your Echo device

As you know, Amazon Echo devices are basically loudspeakers. But Alexa gives them the wisdom to render other digital assistance. Being speakers, they serve to amplify and refines music. So, to optimize your enjoyment of these devices, you'd do well to subscribe to the Family Plan on Amazon Music Unlimited.

If you have the plan, when you finish creating a voice profile on Alexa, you'll find a popup on your screen, giving the option to link your profile to the Music Unlimited account. You'll, of course, take the option, by entering your details of your music account. When you want to play songs, you tell Alexa to play music, and it'll oblige with tunes curated to your taste.

If everyone in the house sets up unique voice profiles, each person will be able to hear music customized to their tastes, according to their selections. Each person can make phone calls from their unique contacts list, and hear news from the sources they chose. Indeed, the Amazon Echo-Alexa partnership helps spice up life in very significant ways.

Connect your Echo device to Bluetooth speaker

The smaller and cheaper Echo Dot came out with the option to connect to a Bluetooth. But Amazon initially thought the bigger and more expensive models didn't need to be connected to extra speakers via Bluetooth.

So, the original Echo didn't come with Bluetooth connectivity. Gladly, you can now connect nearly all of Echo devices with standalone Bluetooth speakers, to get the quantity and quality of audio output you desire for any occasion.

It's pretty easy to pair an Echo device to any Bluetooth speaker you want. Below is how you go about doing that:

- To begin, put your Bluetooth speaker in pairing mode
- Then, open the **Alexa app** on your smartphone or tablet
- Choose **Settings**
- Tape the name of your Echo device model, say, Echo Dot
- Select **Bluetooth**
- Tap on **Pair a New Device**

Once your external speaker shows up on the app, tap on it and give Alexa some moments to pair both devices and confirm to you that the pairing had succeeded.

When your Echo device is paired to a Bluetooth speaker, it means that both equipment will be connected as long as the Echo device is turned on. But you can dissolve the marriage yourself, by un-pairing them when you want to change the speaker or return to the normal Echo device speaker.

What you'll do is:

- Return to the Bluetooth menu on your Alexa mobile app
- Choose the external speaker that is paired to your Echo device

- Select **Forget Device**.

It's that simple. The Echo will actually forget your Bluetooth speaker. But you can pair them again if you have reason to do so.

Chapter 3

20 Alexa skills you can access with Amazon Echo devices

The Alexa in your Echo device never gets tired or feel overworked. It's got hundreds of thousands of app-like abilities called 'skills', and even that vast amount of skills keep growing by the day. Your knowledge of the possibilities only limits the support you can get from Alexa's intelligence.

Amazon has tried to group Alexa skills under 23 broad categories, with each category containing thousands of skills, and counting. The skills come under:

1. Business and Finance
2. Communications
3. Connected car
4. Education and Reference
5. Food and Drinks
6. Games and Trivia
7. Health and Fitness
8. Home Services
9. Kids
10. Lifestyle

11. Local
12. Movies and TV shows
13. Music and Audio
14. News
15. Novelty and Humor
16. Productivity
17. Shopping
18. Smart Home
19. Social
20. Sports
21. Travel and Transportation
22. Utilities
23. Weather

Under these broad classifications, Alexa skill developers have piled thousands of things that you can do with your Amazon Echo devices or, indeed, any Alexa-enabled equipment.

To use most of these skills, you've got to download or set them up, almost the same way you download and install apps on your smartphones, tablets or PCs.

How to add Alexa skills

Just as you download apps into your smartphones, tablets and PCs, you can install any Alexa skill on your Echo Dot or any other Alexa-enabled device. What you do is:

- Open the Alexa app on your smartphone
- Tap on the **Menu** icon, three lines top left of your screen
- On the menu list, choose **Skills & Games**
- If you know the right skill you want to add, search it out. Otherwise, tap **Discover** and begin to browse and review skill descriptions to choose which skill you'll like to add

- When you select a skill, tap **Enable to use**, and that's all. You can proceed to tell Alexa what to do for you based on this skill.

Let's assume you selected *Ocean Sounds Alexa skill* to play some soothing tunes to help you fall asleep after a hectic daily routine; you can say *"Alexa, open Ocean sounds,"* then, relax and enjoy calming tones that'll surely usher restful night sleep.

Manage your Synchrony Bank account with Amazon store Card skill

Join up as we check out at least one Alexa skill from each of the 23 categories, starting with the Amazon Store Card that enables you to manage your Synchrony Bank credit card by simply telling Alexa what to do. That comes under the Business & Finance group of Alexa skills.

Since you already have Alexa app on your smartphone, you can easily add your Synchrony Bank or Capital One accounts so you can conveniently track them, with mere voice commands to Alexa on your Echo device.

- Open the Alexa app and go to **Skills**
- Search for **Amazon Store Card**,
- Enable it and accept the conditions given
- Enter your Synchrony Bank username & password for Amazon store card
- When prompted, create your voice key
- Get started right away, by saying, "Alexa, open store card".

Thenceforth, you can manage your Synchrony Bank credit card by only talking to your tireless digital helper, Miss Alexa.

i. *Alexa, when is my payment due*
ii. *Alexa, did my payment go through*
iii. *Alexa, what's my minimum payment*
iv. *Alexa, what did I buy recently*
v. *Alexa, how much did I spend at Walmart last weekend*
vi. *Alexa, how much did I spend in the last 7 days*
vii. *Alexa, what's my account summary*
viii. *Alexa, what's my remaining credit.*

With conversations like this, you can conveniently keep track of your credit activities, and even seek help on personal finance problems, without lifting a finger. What an exciting time to live!!

Enable Alexa to manage your Capital One accounts on Echo device

If you have Capital One account, you can also track your spending and make payments with your voice, if you give your account information to Alexa. And this is how you do it:

- Launch Alexa app on your smartphone or tablet
- Select Skills
- Browse or search Capital One
- Choose Enable and Accept terms
- Enter the Capital One username & password
- Create your voice key

Right away, you can, you call up Alexa and tell her "Alexa, open Capital One. Alexa, what's my credit balance; Alexa, how much do I have in my savings? You'll receive answers from Alexa, just by asking.

Ordering Pizza through Alexa on your Echo device

Your ability to order and receive Pizza from nearby Pizzeria, without moving an inch from your home, and without even lifting a finger, may not sound like a dramatic leap in human achievement.

Not until you reflect on what it used to be in the past, when you needed to be physically present to get anything at all from the stores. With Alexa and the machines that host her, you can just sit in your living and order pizza with your voice.

You already have an Echo device; go ahead and set up *Pizza Hut or Domino Alexa skill*, linking the account to your Pizza Profile.

- Open the Alexa app

- Select **Skills**

- Search **Pizza Hut Alexa Skill**

- Tap to **Enable** the skill

You'll be prompted to link your Pizza Hut account, which you do if you already have one. Otherwise, you'll have to create one right there on

Alexa app. After, you'll enter email address and password. Once your account is linked, pronto, you can begin voice interaction with your digital assistant.

You can say, Alexa, open Pizza hut

Alexa, ask Pizza hut to place order

Alexa, ask Pizza hut to re-order

When re-ordering, you'll expect Alexa to order precisely the type of pizza you got previously. But if you ask Alexa to place a new order, you'll get the options for pizza types or toppings, and choices of soda.

Pizza Hut Alexa skill also gives you options of how to pay, either by cash or credit card. Of course, credit card payment and home delivery are the way to go with Pizza Hut. You might as well add your card information on your Pizza Hut account to save time.

How to connect your smart home devices to Amazon Echo

Smart home appliances have gone far beyond the Philip Hue lighting bulbs. You now have a motley of home tools designed to obey your voice instructions through Alexa. These include smart door locks, speakers, televisions, thermostats, microwaves, vacuums, security systems, printers, cameras, plugs and many more.

There are two ways to add a smart home device to Alexa so you can operate it with voice. You can use guided discovery, or add the smart home skill along the line of what we discussed above on how to add Alexa skills. But before you begin to try either of the steps,

- Verify that the device is, indeed, Alexa-compatible
- Follow the manufacturer's guidelines to complete smart home setup on the company's app or website
- Hook the home device to the same Wi-Fi network that supports your Echo device
- Check for and install software updates for your smart home equipment.

We'd assume you've checked and confirmed everything to be in order. This is how you do it.

Use guided discovery to enable a smart home device on Alexa

- Open the Alexa app
- Tap the menu icon under time, top left of your screen
- Select **Add Device**
- Choose the type of home device you want to add
- Select the brand and follow on-screen guidelines to finish the connection

Once you've connected the device, you sit back and say, for instance, *"Alexa, turn off the lights in the bedroom,"* or *"Alexa, reduce thermostat by 3 degrees."*

Use Alexa skill to catch up on the news (Set up Flash Briefings)

Agreed, there're a thousand and one ways to catch up on the news these days. Besides the traditional radio, television and newspapers, you now have social platforms like Facebook, Twitter, and YouTube and others. But you don't have one thousand and one hours to get your news update.

- As always, open the Alexa app on your mobile phone
- Tap on the menu icon, and select **Settings**
- Choose **Flash Briefing**. You'll see many supported news services

- Tap on the toggle next to each news source you want to be getting updates from.

The news services you can enable are many, including Bloomberg, Associated Press, Slate, The Daily News and Wall Street Journal. Afterwards, you can say, "Alexa, what is in the news," or "Alexa, what is my Flash Briefing."

With a very query to Alexa on your Echo device, you can listen to news updates while preparing dinner, while having breakfast, or even while driving to work. Alexa makes you squeeze more beneficial activities within your limited time.

Setup calling & messaging skill in Alexa communication

Under your Alexa skills Communications category, you can enable the digital assistant to help you make calls and send text messages on your mobile phone by voice. You only need to take three short steps to achieve that feat.

- On the Alexa app page, tap on the menu icon
- Select **Skills and Advance**
- Choose **Communicate**
- Verify your smartphone details, then grant permissions to Alexa for calling and messaging

- If you like, import your contact list when asked to do so. Although this is optional, it's something that you'll want to do because it makes life easier for you.

When you've taken these steps, you can say:

Ale<u>x</u>a, call John's Echo (Echo to Echo call)

Alexa, call Juliet on her home phone

Alexa, Call Grandma

Alexa, Mary's office line

It's important to note that Alexa voice calls do not yet support emergency service numbers like 911. It also does not support toll-free numbers, abbreviated three-digit code numbers like 211 and calls outside of the United States and its territories.

Set up your Uber account so Alexa can get you a ride

Everyone knows just how easy it's to get a taxi ride through the Uber app. Alexa has made it even more comfortable, such that you just give a voice command to the tireless digital helper, and the taxi is on the way. But you have to add your Uber account on your Echo device.

- As usual, open **the Alexa app** on your smartphone
- Tap the **menu icon** on the upper left
- Select **Skills** and search for Uber skill
- Tap to Enable the feature
- Sign in to your Uber account. In the Device Location, set your home or

office as the most likely you'll be when needing a taxi.

When you're done setting up the platform, you can tell Alexa what to do each time you need a ride.

You can say, for instance:

Alexa, get me UberSUV ride

Alexa, ask Uber for a ride

Alexa, ask Uber to request Uberselect

Alexa, ask Uber the position of my taxi

Get your Sports Scores on Echo through voice request to Alexa

One Alexa skill that appeals to sports lovers is **Sports Update** skill. With the help of Alexa, you can keep up with the scores of your favorite league competitions, both finished games and those in progress. But you've got to be sure the league you want to follow, is supported by Alexa skill.

You'll be glad to know that all major sports leagues in the United States are supported, including the NBA, the

MLB, NCAA, NFL, the National Hockey League, and the WNBA. The popular English Premier League, the Football Association Challenge Cup, the German Bundesliga and UEFA Champions League are among the big leagues which scores you can follow, by merely asking Alexa to tell you.

To enable this exciting feature to be used on your Echo Dot or any other Alexa host device:

- Open the Alexa app on your smartphone
- Tap on the 3-line menu icon top-left of the screen
- Choose Settings
- Select Sport Update

- Use the search window to find the teams you want to follow
- Tap to add the team to your favorite teams' list
- You can add or remove teams at will, and when you're done setting up the feature, you can say:

Alexa, give me a sports update

Alexa, what's the score of New York Yankees game

Alexa, when do the Dallas Mavericks play next?

Alexa, who's winning in the LA Lakers game

Alexa, what's the score of Arsenal game

Monitor the Stock Market

If you're an investor in the stock, you'll the Alexa skill called Fidelity Investments. It's a feature that helps to track or trade on the stock market anytime and from anywhere, just by telling Alexa what you want to do. When you enable this skill on your Echo device, you can ask Alexa to tell you the latest prices of the equities you're watching. You'll get real-time market updates and stock quotes through voice interaction with Alexa.

You can sit back and tell Alexa to enable this handy skill for you. You could say, *"Alexa, enable Fidelity"*. And she will do it for you.

Remember that Alexa can equally help you to activate all the other skills we've discussed before, or other ones you may want to use. But if you choose to set up the Fidelity Investment skill yourself, this is how you'll do it:

- Open the Alexa app
- Tap the menu icon at the upper left of the screen
- Scroll down to **Settings**
- Select **Skills & Advance**
- Browse or search Fidelity Investment and toggle the button next to it. Then, you can begin to ask questions

about all the publicly quoted companies in the country.

Right away, you can say, for instance:

Alexa, ask Fidelity how Amazon is doing

Alexa, what's the price of Google stock

Alexa, ask Fidelity for a quote on Amazon Alexa

How to Track your packages with Alexa

Waiting for packages you ordered from Amazon, or those coming UPS or U.S. Service or FedEx isn't always a beautiful experience. This is not saying that these agencies have a poor reputation in delivery services.

It's just that waiting for stuffs always seems to stretch to eternity, no matter how short they actually take to arrive. Part of the problem is, you're in the dark, since there's usually no real time information concerning the position of the package.

It's gladsome that Amazon Echo owners are now able to track their orders by asking "Alexa, where is my package." You no longer need to pick up your phone and place a call, or hit the computer keyboard, so that you can track a package you bought from Amazon. Alexa can now help you keep an eye on the package and keep you informed about its movement. Necessary as this skill is, it was initially limited to Amazon dispatches.

Over time, Alexa gained new skills that now work with other carriers. These include the **UPS skill**, which lets you know if you have packages on the way, the nearest UPS office to your location and how you can know the shipping cost. This skill will work for you, only if you sign up for **My Choice account** on the UPS website.

Similarly, you need to sign up for an **Informed Delivery account** of the U.S. Postal Service before you can enjoy Alexa tracking ability for packages sent from the Post Office.

If you enable Alexa for the postal service, you'll be able to ask Alexa, when will my package arrive, how many packages will arrive on Wednesday.

To enable this exciting skill,

- Open the Alexa app on a smartphone
- Tap the Menu icon (the 3-line located top left of your page
- Select **Settings,** then **Notifications**, and **Shopping Notifications**
- Here, you've got 4 options. You can toggle on all of them, if you want, or just one or two.

For instance, you can toggle on **Delivery Notification**, so Alexa will send you information when your package is out for delivery and when it's dropped at your doorsteps. Tap to enable **Give product names, where is my stuff**, and Alexa will be telling you the items in the pack and its position. And you can enable **Reorder notification** so Alexa to receive information about ordering pieces of stuff you've ordered before.

You'll be asking Alexa,

Where is my stuff

Alexa, track my stuff

Alexa, reorder baby wipes from Amazon

Alexa, ask Post Office how many packages will I get on Wednesday?

Alexa, ask UPS how can I know the shipping cost of 2 oz. package

Alexa, ask UPS if I have packages on the way

Secure your Alexa privacy

You know that Alexa makes a recording of all your queries and interfaces with her. That could be scary, especially if you sometimes ask embarrassing questions. You'll not cherish the idea of having all that saved up for too long. Gladly, you can swiftly delete individual conversations shortly after they occur.

- Go to **Settings**
- Select **Alexa Privacy**
- Select a particular recording
- Tap on **Delete voice recording**

Additionally, you can delete all your voice recording for the day, week, or month. You can even wipe clean everything ever recorded on your Alexa account.

Still in the Privacy section, you can set up your device to automatically delete your voice recordings.

Try meditation with Alexa on Echo device

You may have heard that skilful meditation can help you manage stress. Amazon Echo device, with your loyal assistant, Alexa, can take you through some controlled meditation will surely calm your frayed nerves.

You can find meditation skills under the **Health & Fitness** category of Alexa skills and also under **Lifestyles.** If you do not want to personally search out, review and enable specific meditation skills, you can tell Alexa to suggest one for you, each time you want to relax.

And if you know some, like Headspace, Sweet Dreams or Guided Meditation, you can simply tell Alexa to open them, each time you want to indulge in any one of them.

You can say, for instance, Alexa, open Headspace. You'll hear a calming voice of virtual Andy who tells you the goodness of meditation. He will then take you through a round of meditation, which you can pause and resume as you want.

You can tell Alexa, "Ask Headspace for meditation to help me wind down". Or, perhaps, "Alexa, tell Headspace I want to sleep." Whatever you want, Alexa will tell Andy, and Andy will dutifully calm you down and lure you to sleep.

Can anyone do without Alexa and her hosts, Amazon Echo devices?

No end to Alexa Skills

There's no end to what Alexa can help you do without lifting a finger. Numerous as they are, it's not hard to find and enable the skills relevant to your daily routine.

In fact, all you need do to reveal the amazing capacities of this artificial intelligence is to wake Alexa and ask her what she can do. You can say, for instance, "Alexa, what can you do."

Or, you can budget time to browse each of the 23 skill categories, pick out a couple of skills in each category; read through their descriptions. You'll be amazed at what Amazon Alexa can do.

And if you'll like to enable any of the skills you discover, you'd not need to follow the manual way of opening the app and tapping icons and toggles. All you need to do is say, "Alexa, enable the Geneva skill." Fiam, you'll get features that let you control **General Electric's Wi-Fi Connect** home appliances with your voice.

But you must buy any of the Echo devices first before you can enjoy the easy life of doing much with mere verbal instructions to Alexa in the Echo.

DISCLAIMER

The author believes users of the **Amazon ECHO DOT** will find this book helpful in understanding **How to use their device**.

However, it is just a small book. It should not be relied upon solely for all ECHO DOT tricks and problems.

ABOUT THE AUTHOR

Brian A. Lake is a software analyst with many years of experience. He has worked with different IT companies all over the world as a consultant developer.

He is actively involved in an ongoing project to enable novice and tech enthusiasts get a deeper understanding of the tech world through his best seller books.

Presently, he works as a freelancer; writing blog posts and articles –with contributions from other tech and gadget gurus in *Dockyard Inc.* - for users to master their electronic device